pages 9-16

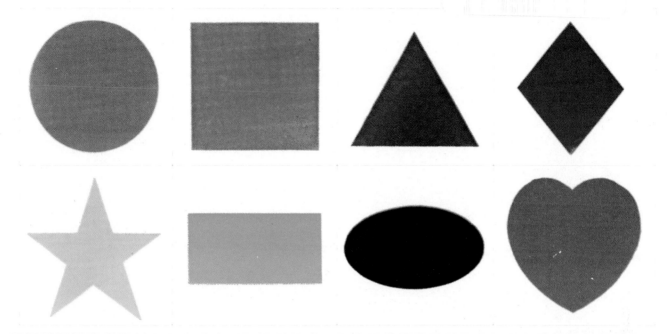

page 17   page 20   page 23

Rewards!   Use these stickers as rewards on any page.

red

blue

<u>Parent</u>: Have your child find the blue sticker, put it in place, and color the rest of the objects blue.

yellow

green

Parent: have your child find the green sticker, put it in place, and color the rest of the objects green.

orange

purple

6   <u>Parent:</u> Have your child find the purple sticker, put it in place, and color the rest of the objects purple.

black

brown

8 <u>Parent:</u> Have your child find the brown sticker, put it in place, and color the rest of the objects brown.

circle

Parent: Have your child find the sticker and color the matching shapes.

9

square

Parent: Have your child find the sticker and color the matching shapes.

triangle

Parent: Have your child find the sticker and color the matching shapes.

11

diamond

Parent: Have your child find the sticker and color the matching shapes.

star

Parent: Have your child find the sticker and color the matching shapes.

13

rectangle

Parent: Have your child find the sticker and color the matching shapes.

oval

heart

Parent: Have your child find the sticker and color the matching shapes.

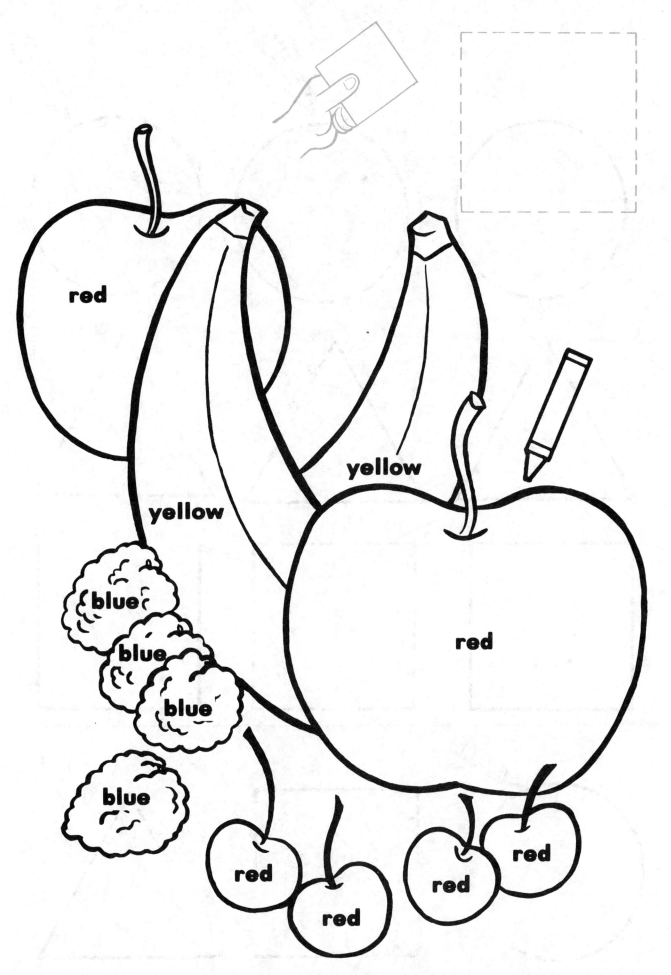

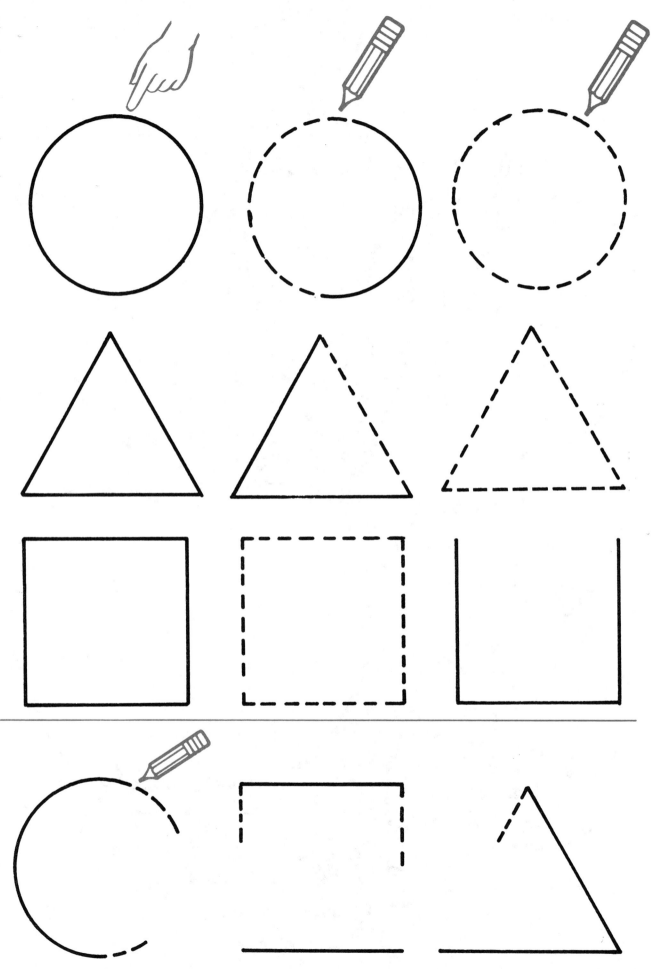

18

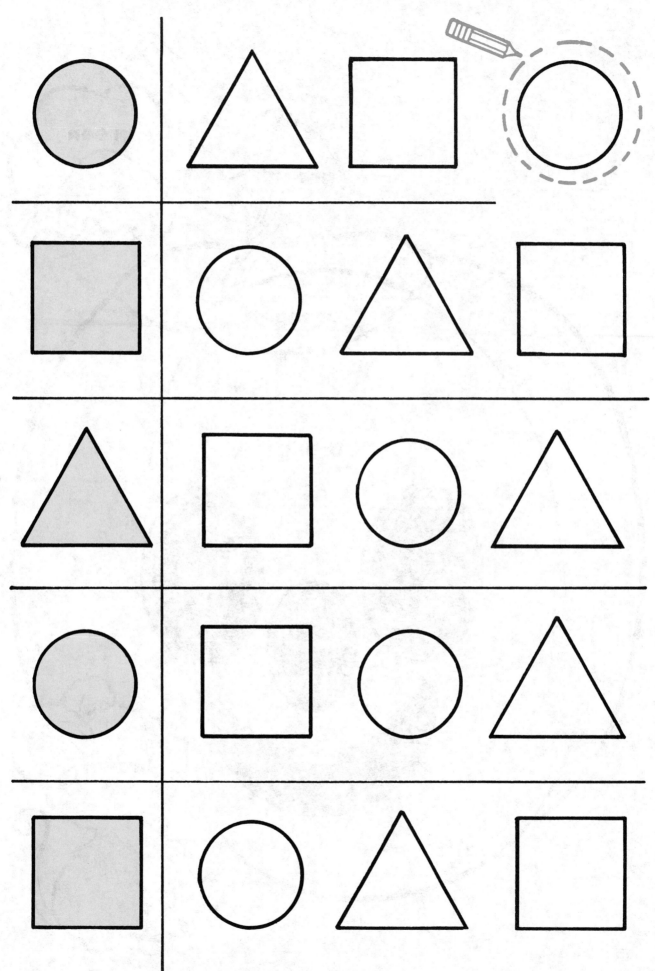

Parent: Have your child find the matching shape in each row and circle it.

19

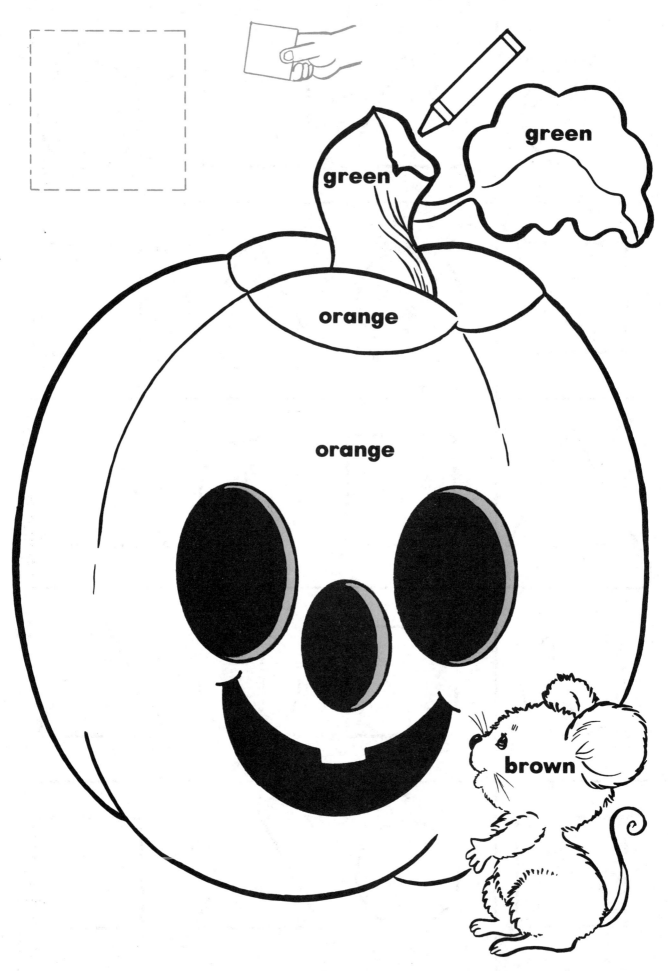

green

green

orange

orange

brown

Parent: Have your child put the sticker in place and color the picture to match it.

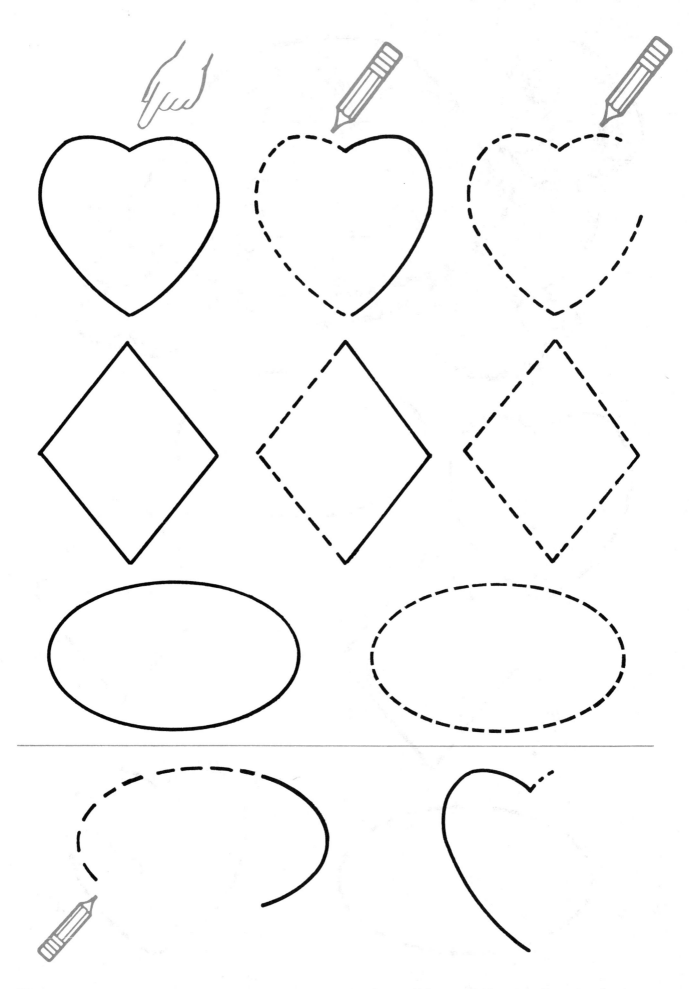

Parent: Help your child trace and complete the shapes.

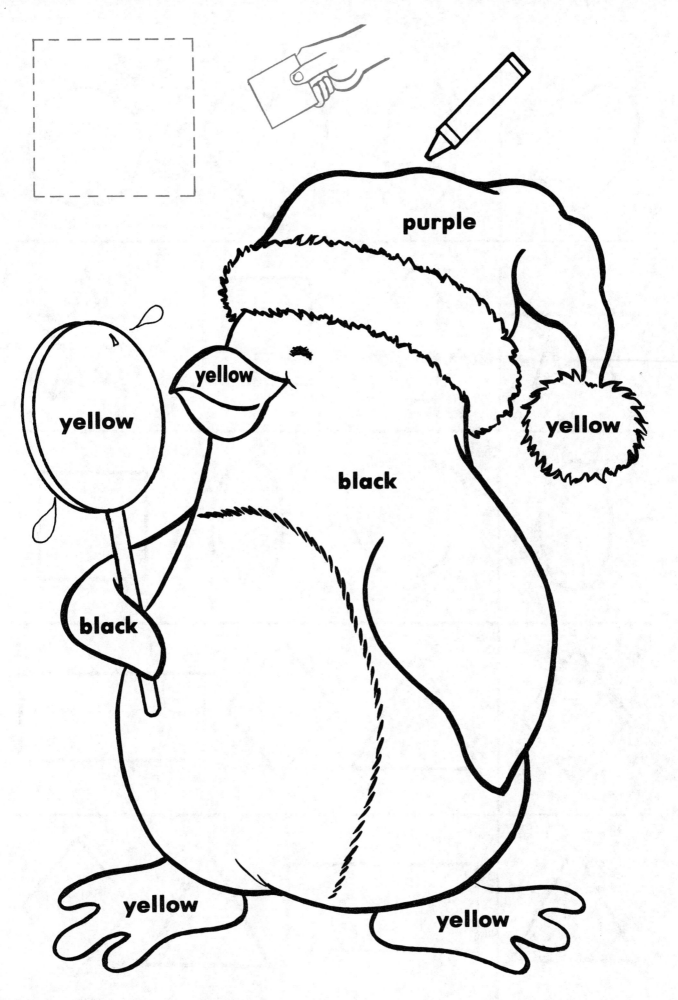

purple

yellow

yellow

yellow

black

black

yellow

yellow

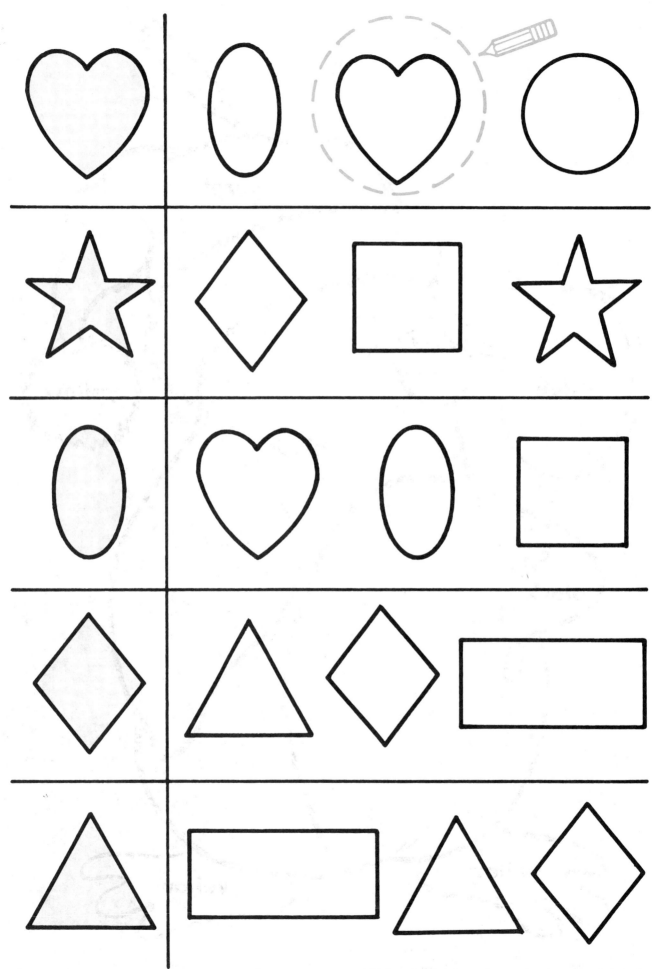

24

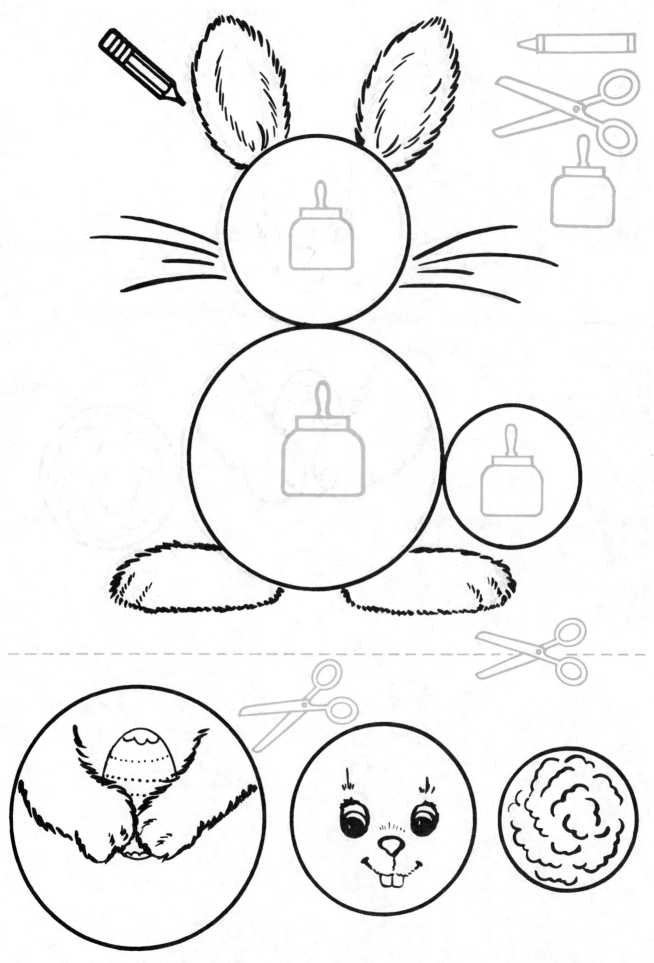

Parent: Help your child color, cut out and paste the shapes in their places.

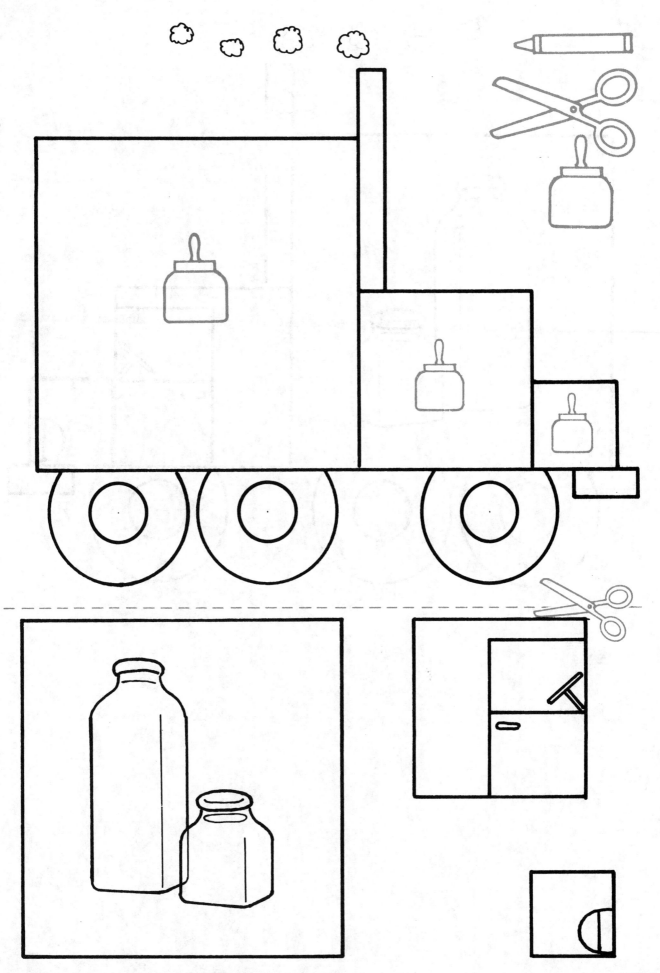

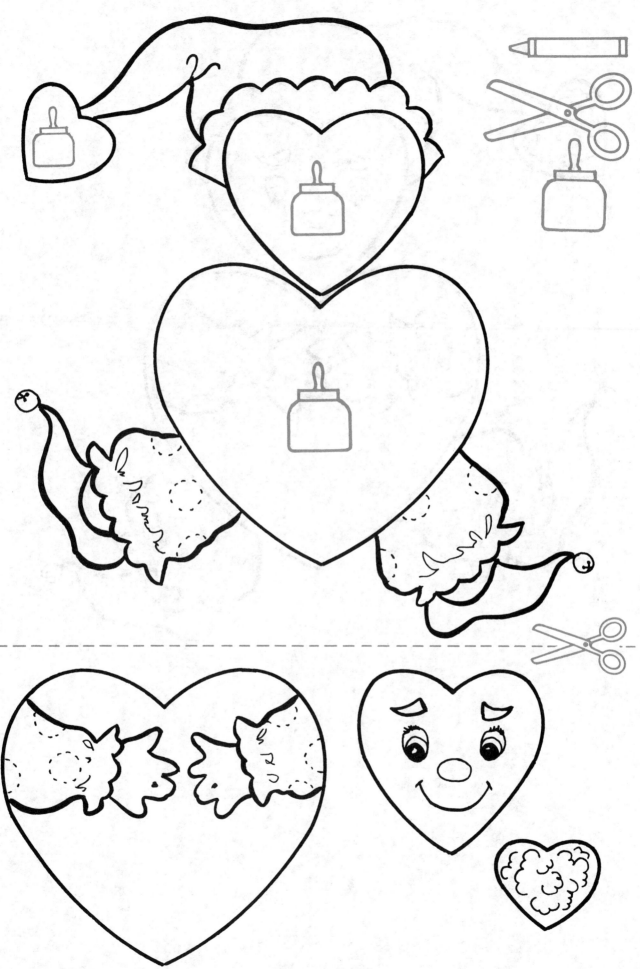

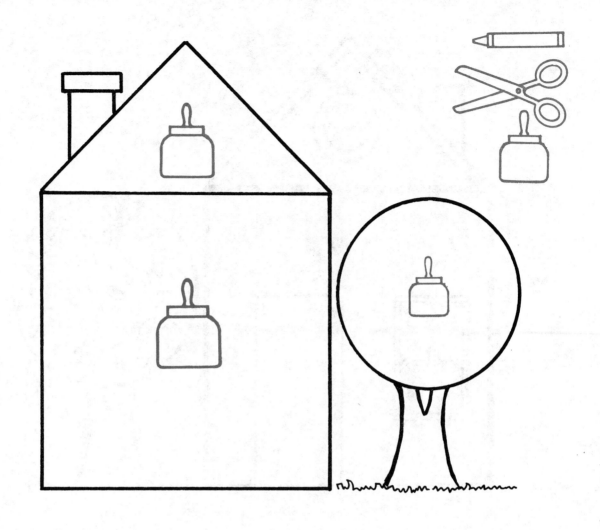

Parent: Help your child color, cut out and paste the shapes in their places.

Shapes and Colors

•Peel off stickers and apply to page.